ANIMALS OF THE GRASSLANDS

DEADLY RHINOCEROSES

THERESA EMMINIZER

PowerKiDS press.
New York

Published in 2021 by The Rosen Publishing Group, Inc.
29 East 21st Street, New York, NY 10010

Portions of this work were authored by Ethan Grucella and published as *Rhinoceroses*. All new material in this edition authored by Theresa Emminizer.

Editor: Theresa Emminizer
Book Design: Michael Flynn

Photo Credits: Cover EcoPrint/Shutterstock.com; p. 5 e2dan/Shutterstock.com; p. 7 (black rhino) PictureMike/Shutterstock.com; p. 7 (white rhino) Mark Bridger/Shutterstock.com; p. 9 Andrea Izzotti/Shutterstock.com; p. 11 AfricaWildlife/Shutterstock.com; p. 13 JMx Images/Shutterstock.com; p. 15 Chris Twine/Shutterstock.com; p. 17 Ivanov Gleb/Shutterstock.com; p. 19 Vladimir Wrangel/Shutterstock.com; p. 21 Poring Studio/Shutterstock.com; p. 22 (black rhino) Svetlana Foote/Shutterstock.com; p. 22 (white rhino) prapass/Shutterstock.com.

Cataloging-in-Publication Data

Names: Emminizer, Theresa.
Title: Deadly rhinoceroses / Theresa Emminizer.
Description: New York : PowerKids Press, 2021. | Series: Animals of the grasslands | Includes glossary and index.
Identifiers: ISBN 9781725316942 (pbk.) | ISBN 9781725316966 (library bound) | ISBN 9781725316959 (6 pack)
Subjects: LCSH: Rhinoceroses–Juvenile literature.
Classification: LCC QL737.U63 E44 2021 | DDC 599.66'8–dc23

Manufactured in the United States of America

CPSIA Compliance Information: Batch #CSPK20. For Further Information contact Rosen Publishing, New York, New York at 1-800-237-9932.

CONTENTS

Rhino Species

There are five species, or kinds, of rhinoceroses. Three species live in Asia. Two species live in the grasslands of Africa. These are the southern white rhino and western black rhino. Although their names might suggest otherwise, they're both actually gray!

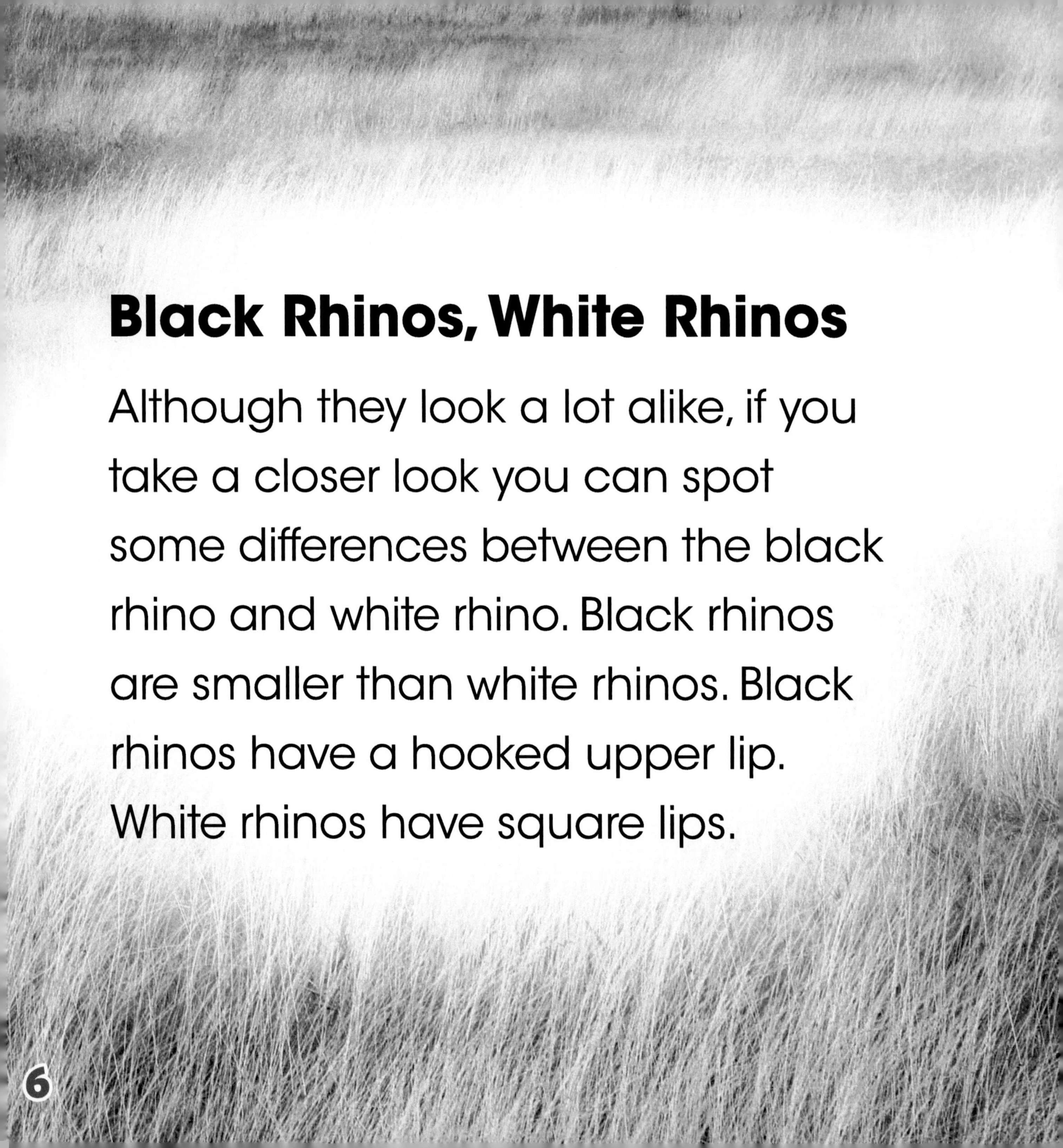

Black Rhinos, White Rhinos

Although they look a lot alike, if you take a closer look you can spot some differences between the black rhino and white rhino. Black rhinos are smaller than white rhinos. Black rhinos have a hooked upper lip. White rhinos have square lips.

black rhino

white rhino

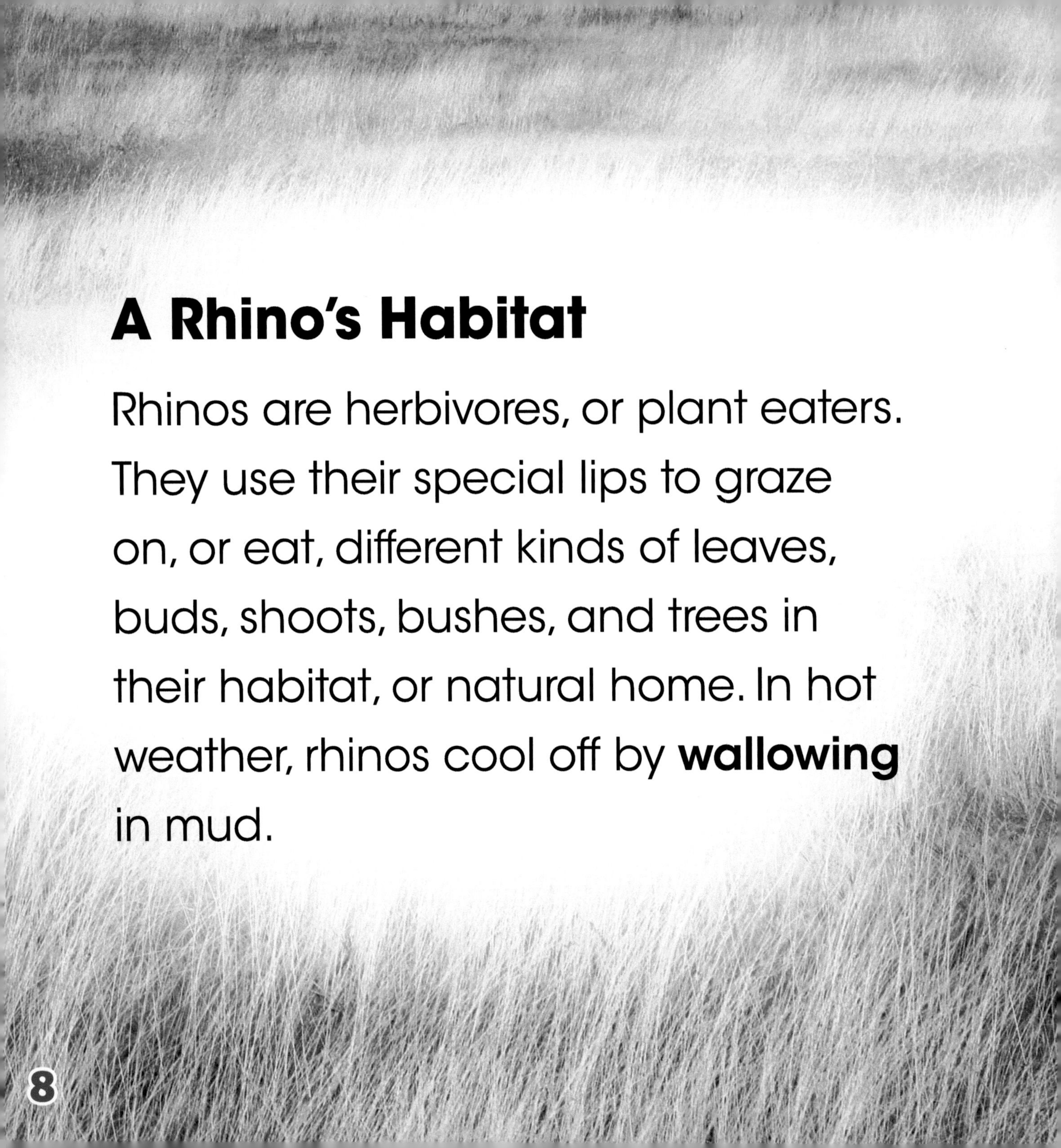

A Rhino's Habitat

Rhinos are herbivores, or plant eaters. They use their special lips to graze on, or eat, different kinds of leaves, buds, shoots, bushes, and trees in their habitat, or natural home. In hot weather, rhinos cool off by **wallowing** in mud.

Unlikely Friends

Rhinos are often seen with birds riding around on their backs! These birds are called oxpeckers. They help rhinos out by eating the bugs that live in rhinos' skin. Oxpeckers also help rhinos by crying out when danger is near.

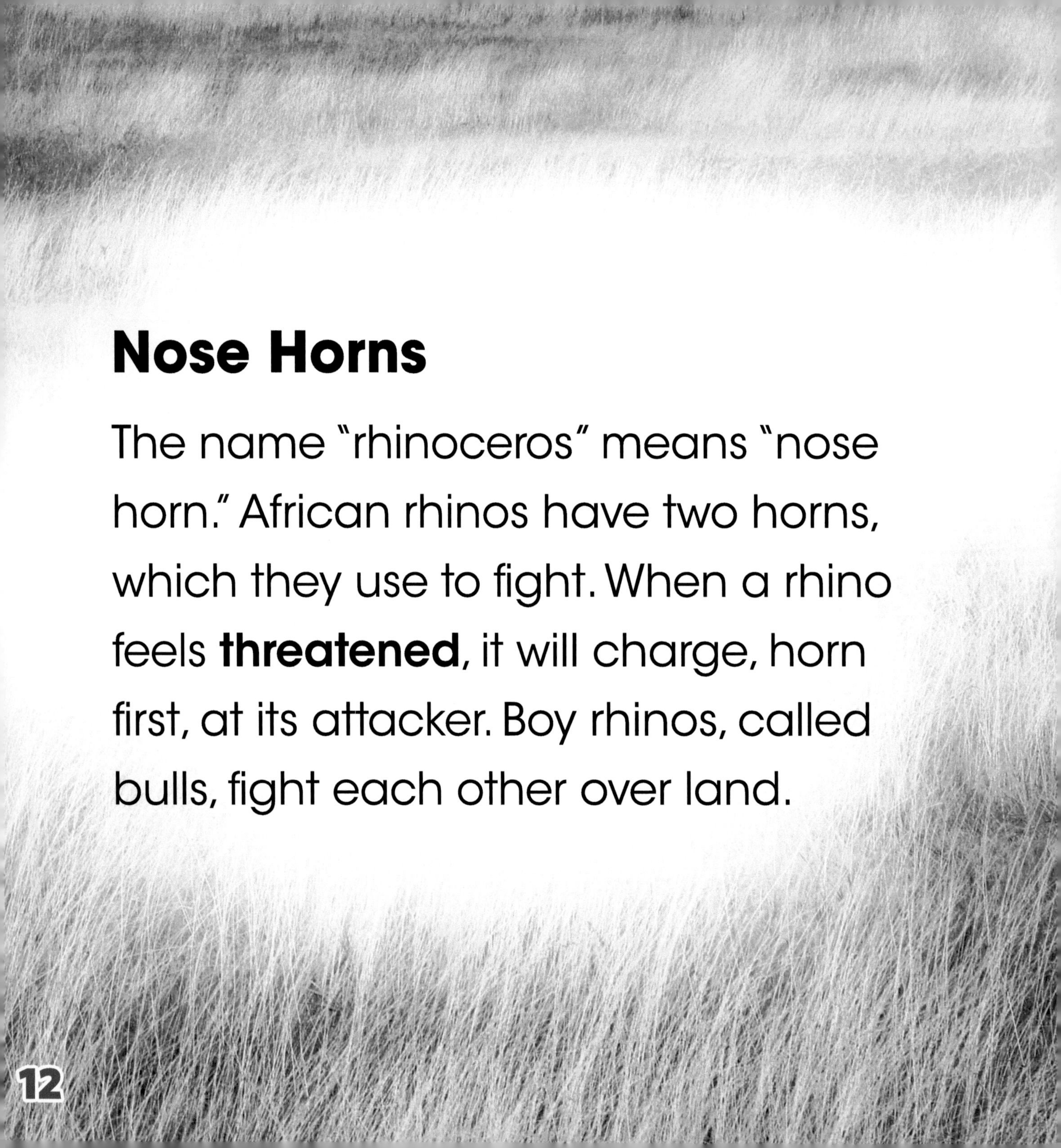

Nose Horns

The name "rhinoceros" means "nose horn." African rhinos have two horns, which they use to fight. When a rhino feels **threatened**, it will charge, horn first, at its attacker. Boy rhinos, called bulls, fight each other over land.

Staying Safe

Because they're so big and strong, rhinos have few natural predators. Predators are animals that hunt other animals for food. Rhinos have thick skin that **protects** them like **armor**. They can run up to 34 miles (55 km) per hour.

A Rhino's Life

Rhinos spend most of their time alone. But sometimes they come together in groups with up to six members. A group of rhinos is called a crash. Rhinos communicate, or talk, with each other by snorting, squeaking, growling, and grunting.

Baby Rhinos

Rhinos mothers carry babies inside their bodies for about 16 months. Baby rhinos are called calves. Rhino calves weigh between 78 and 138 pounds (35 to 63 kg) at birth.

Rhinos at Risk

As human populations rise, rhino habitats are being ruined, meaning rhinos have fewer places to live and eat. Rhinos are also hunted for their horns. Some rhino species are in danger of going extinct, or disappearing completely. Today, most rhinos live within national parks and **reserves**.

Fancy Features

BLACK RHINO

Height: 5.2 feet (1.6 m) at the shoulder

Weight: 1,984–2,976 pounds (900–1,350 kg)

Top Speed: 34 miles (55 km) per hour

WHITE RHINO

Height: 5–6 feet (1.5–1.8 m) at the shoulder

Weight: 3,968–5,511 pounds (1,800–2,500 kg)

Top Speed: 25 miles (40 km) per hour

GLOSSARY

armor: Clothing to help protect the body.

protects: Keeps safe.

reserves: Land set aside for wildlife.

threatened: Likely to be harmed.

wallowing: Rolling around in mud or muddy water.

INDEX

WEBSITES

Due to the changing nature of Internet links, PowerKids Press has developed an online list of websites related to the subject of this book. This site is updated regularly. Please use this link to access the list: www.powerkidslinks.com/aotg/rhinos